WHAT ON EARTH IS HAPPENING?

SIGNS OF THE TIMES SERIES

VAL WALDECK

Copyright © 2016, Val Waldeck
All Rights Reserved

Cover design by Clive Thompson
www.getclive.com

All scripture quotations, unless otherwise indicated, are taken from the New King James Version of the Bible. Copyright © 1982 by Thomas Nelson, Inc. Used with permission. All rights reserved.

Dedication

Dedicated to all who are "looking for the blessed hope and glorious appearing of our great God and Savior Jesus Christ,"
Titus 2:13

TABLE OF CONTENTS

WHAT ON EARTH IS HAPPENING?......1

Val Waldeck 1

Dedication 3

Table of Contents 5

Preface 7

Chapter 1
World events and The Return of Jesus 11

Chapter 2
The Promise of His Return is an Attested Scriptural Truth 13

Chapter 3
Scoffers in the Last Days 19

Chapter 4
The Certainty of His Return 21

Chapter 5
Political Turmoil 23

Chapter 6
The Explosion of Knowledge 25

Chapter 7
The Coming World Ruler 29

Chapter 8
The One-World Government 33

Chapter 9
The One-World Religion 41

Chapter 10
The One World Economy 51

Chapter 11
The Call to be Ready 57

A special prayer for those who need Christ 61

About The Author 63

Disclaimer 64

More Books by Val 65

Preface

We are living in one of the most exciting periods of this world's history. Time, as we know it, is rapidly drawing to a close as the COMING OF THE LORD draws near. All over the world people are aware that something is happening.

This is the age of fulfilment of Biblical prophecy and, for the discerning believer, our local newspapers bear testimony to that fact daily.

Before 1900 very few commentaries were written on prophetical books such as Daniel and Revelation. It was not easy in those days to understand, for example, how something lodged in the human body would enable a person to "buy and sell."

> *"He causes all, both small and great, rich and poor, free and slave, to receive a mark on their right hand or on their foreheads, and that no one may buy or sell except one who has the mark or the name of the beast, or the number of his name.*
> *Here is wisdom. Let him who has understanding calculate the number of the beast, for it is the number of a man: His number is 666."*
> Revelation 13:16-18

This Scripture written over two thousand years ago by the Apostle John on the Isle of Patmos has had people puzzled for ages. What kind of mark is this? How is it placed in the human body? And what does it have to do with commerce?

Today we have the answer to all those questions. We know about modern technology and microchips. We chip our animals, motor cars and possessions, which links them to computers so they may be easily trace. We have heard about the future of credit cards being replaced by computer chips in the bodies of people which will enable them to conduct commerce with the use of scanners, among other things.

Isn't it interesting that the 666 is the binary code used by computer programmers? Every barcode uses the 666 format.

What about the possibility of the whole world simultaneously viewing an event in Jerusalem?

> *"When they finish their testimony, the beast that ascends out of the bottomless pit will make war against them, overcome them, and kill them. And their dead bodies will lie in the street of the great city which spiritually is called Sodom and Egypt, where also our Lord was crucified. Then those from the peoples, tribes, tongues, and nations will see their dead bodies three-and-a-half days, and not allow their dead bodies to be put into graves. And those who dwell on the earth will rejoice over them, make merry, and send gifts to one another, because these two prophets tormented those who dwell on the earth."*
> *Now after the three-and-a-half days the breath of life from God entered them, and they stood on their feet, and great fear fell on those who saw them.*
> *And they heard a loud voice from heaven saying to them, "Come up here." And they ascended to heaven in a cloud, and their enemies saw them."*
> Revelation 11:7-12

The Old Testament prophet, Daniel, wrote that end-time prophecy would be more clearly understood as knowledge increases in the last days and that is an exciting fact.

> *"But you, Daniel, shut up the words, and seal the book until the time of the end; many shall run to and fro, and knowledge shall increase... Go your way, Daniel, for the words are closed up and sealed till the time of the end.*
> Daniel. 12:4,9

As historical events unfold THE SIGNS OF THE TIMES are evident for all who will see.

> *"But you, brethren, are not in darkness, so that this Day should overtake you as a thief."*
> 1 Thessalonians 5:4

The Lord Jesus Christ put it this way:

> *"Now when these things begin to happen, look up and lift up your heads, because your redemption draws near."*
> Luke 21:28

Val Waldeck

Durban, South Africa.

Email: val@valwaldeck.com

Website: www.valwaldeck.com

Chapter 1

World events and the Return of Jesus

The Bible is a prophetic book. It speaks of historical events in the lives of people and nations with a certainty and clarity that is unique.

Thousands of years before they existed, in many cases, the destinies of individuals and nations were charted with precision and history bears out the accuracy of those predictions. Its prophecies are being fulfilled right up to the present time and we read about them daily in our newspapers.

This is not surprising when one considers the amazing miracle that we call "The Bible."

The Bible is actually a collection of sixty-six books, written over a period of 1600 years, spanning 60 generations. Many of the approximately 40 authors involved did not know each other or enjoy the privilege of reading one another's work. They came from all walks of life and wrote at different times, on three continents (Asia, Africa and Europe), in three languages (Hebrew, Aramaic and Greek), and about hundreds of different and often controversial subjects.

These inspired writings were collated and compiled into one Book and the signature of Almighty Eternal God can be clearly seen. There is one underlying theme from Genesis in the Old Testament to the book of Revelation in the New Testament — the coming of the Saviour to pay the price of sin... and His Return to bring a climax to this world's history.

The "*Holy Scriptures, which are able to make you wise for salvation through faith in Christ Jesus*" (2 Timothy 3:15) also tells us that "*Christ was offered once to bear the sins of many. To those who eagerly wait for Him He will appear a second time, apart from sin, for salvation.*" (Hebrews 9:28).

Those who have seriously investigated the Bible's prophetic, scientific and historical accuracy are left in no doubt that the predictions concerning the Return of Jesus Christ to our world will be just as precisely fulfilled. It cannot be otherwise.

World events — the prophesied "Signs of the Times" — should make mankind sit up and take note. Everything is going according to the Divine Plan and His Return is on schedule.

Sadly, however, the comment of Jesus rings true, even in our generation.

"When it is evening you say, 'It will be fair weather, for the sky is red'; and in the morning, 'It will be foul weather today, for the sky is red and threatening.' Hypocrites! You know how to discern the face of the sky, but you cannot discern the signs of the times."
Matthew 16:2-3

Chapter 2

The Promise of His Return is an Attested Scriptural Truth

It is estimated that there are more than three hundred prophecies in the Bible concerning the first coming of Christ ... and about eight times as many concerning His Second Coming. The New Testament mentions it at least 318 times in 210 chapters and there can be no doubt that saints throughout the ages have always "looked for His appearing."

This is no new doctrine dreamed up by some feverish theological brain. Even that Old Testament saint, Enoch — just seven generations from Adam — looked way beyond his time and prophesied concerning the Second Coming of Christ. This godly man, who walked so close to the Lord that he just walked right into His Presence one day (Genesis 5:22), said: *"Behold, the Lord comes with ten thousands of His saints"* (Jude verse 14).

The inspired Scriptures tell us that the Lord Jesus Christ will return personally in a literal and visible manner.

> *"And while they looked steadfastly toward heaven as He went up, behold, two men stood by them in white apparel, who also said, 'Men of Galilee, why do you stand gazing up into heaven? This same Jesus, who was taken up from you*

> *into heaven, will so come in like manner*
> *as you saw Him go into heaven."*
> Acts 1:10-11

Genuine Christians will be the first to meet Him.

> *"But I do not want you to be ignorant, brethren,*
> *concerning those who have fallen asleep,*
> *lest you sorrow as others who have no hope.*
> *For if we believe that Jesus died and rose again,*
> *even so God will bring with Him those who sleep in Jesus.*
> *For this we say to you by the word of the Lord,*
> *that we who are alive and remain until the coming of the Lord*
> *will by no means precede those who are asleep.*
> *For the Lord Himself will descend from heaven with a shout, with the voice*
> *of an archangel, and with the trumpet of God.*
> *And the dead in Christ will rise first.*
> *Then we who are alive and remain shall be caught up together*
> *with them in the clouds to meet the Lord in the air.*
> *And thus we shall always be with the Lord.*
> *Therefore comfort one another with these words."*
> 1 Thessalonians 4:13-18

We notice that those who love the Lord, and have died before His return, will come back with Him. The atoms that made up their bodies will be called together and they will receive their resurrection bodies at exactly the same time as believers currently living on the earth. Together ... we shall be caught up in the clouds to meet the Lord in the air.

This "catching up" of the saints is what is known as "The Rapture of the Church". This is the first phase of the Second Coming. Those who do not know the Lord will not see Him at this time. Their turn is coming.

The second phase occurs when the Lord — together with all His saints — returns and stands physically on the Mount of Olives in Jerusalem – the very place He left this earth after He came the first time.

Zechariah 14:4 tells us about it.

> *"And in that day His feet will stand on the Mount of Olives,*
> *which faces Jerusalem on the east.*
> *And the Mount of Olives shall be split in two from east to west,*
> *making a very large valley;*
> *Half of the mountain shall move toward the north*
> *And half of it toward the south."*
> Zechariah 14:4

It will happen suddenly and unexpectedly as far as the world is concerned.

> *"But concerning the times and the seasons, brethren,*
> *you have no need that I should write to you.*
> *For you yourselves know perfectly that the day of the Lord*
> *so comes as a thief in the night.*
> *For when they say, "Peace and safety!" then sudden destruction*
> *comes upon them, as labor pains upon a pregnant woman.*
> *And they shall not escape."*
> 1 Thessalonians 5:1-3

Everybody will know about it — from the East to the West.

> *"For as the lightning comes from the east and flashes to the west,*
> *so also will the coming of the Son of Man be."*
> *Matthew 24:27"*

The Book of Revelation gives us some more detail:

> *"Behold, He is coming with clouds, and every eye will see Him,*
> *even they who pierced Him.*
> *And all the tribes of the earth will mourn because of Him.*
> *Even so, Amen."*
> Revelation 1:7

The sight of the Glorious Resurrected Christ will shock this world.

> *"Then the sign of the Son of Man will appear in heaven,*
> *and then all the tribes of the earth will mourn,*
> *and they will see the Son of Man coming*
> *on the clouds of heaven with power and great glory."*
> Matthew 24:30

Terrified, those who once scoffed and mocked will call out to the mountains and the rocks:

> *"Fall on us and hide us from the face of Him who sits on the throne*
> *and from the wrath of the Lamb!"*
> Revelation 6:16

There is a Day coming when every individual and nation will acknowledge the Lord Jesus Christ to be King of Kings and Lord of Lords.

> *"…that at the name of Jesus every knee should bow,*
> *of those in heaven, and of those on earth, and of those under the earth,*
> *and that every tongue should confess that Jesus Christ is Lord,*
> *to the glory of God the Father."*
> Philippians 2:10-11

When Christ returns, every knee will bow — willingly or unwillingly. What a joy to bow before Him now and enjoy wonderful fellowship with the Risen Lord while we wait for His Return.

Chapter 3

Scoffers in the Last Days

Noah spent 120 years building his ark... and people scoffed right until the moment the floods came and washed them all away.

Jesus said it would be just like "the days of Noah" when He returns. People will be concerned with their daily lives and totally unconcerned about the calamity about to befall them. The words of the prophets will, once again, fall on deaf ears.

Nearly two thousand years ago, Peter wrote that this would be so. Those who scoff are merely fulfilling prophecy and, in fact, become a prophetic sign themselves pointing to the soon return of the Lord.

> *"...knowing this first: that scoffers will come in the last days, walking according to their own lusts, and saying, "Where is the promise of His coming? For since the fathers fell asleep, all things continue as they were from the beginning of creation."*
> 2 Peter 3:3-4

Mockers have forgotten that the Lord always fulfils His Word. He spoke "in the beginning" and the worlds came into being.

He spoke again and floods destroyed the earth. His same Word is preserving the world right now for the Final Judgment.

> *"For this they willfully forget: that by the word of God the heavens were of old, and the earth standing out of water and in the water, by which the world that then existed perished, being flooded with water. But the heavens and the earth which are now preserved by the same word, are reserved for fire until the day of judgment and perdition of ungodly men."*
> 2 Peter 3:5-7

As far as God is concerned, time is but a fleeting moment. It is like a puff of smoke in the light of Eternity.

> *"…whereas you do not know what will happen tomorrow. For what is your life? It is even a vapor that appears for a little time and then vanishes away."*
> James 4:14

God has graciously given mankind this time in which to repent and turn to Him because of His great love for us. Our merciful God is not willing that anyone should perish without hope. It may be possible to live without Christ in this world, but to die without Him is the greatest of all tragedies.

> *"But, beloved, do not forget this one thing, that with the Lord one day is as a thousand years, and a thousand years as one day. The Lord is not slack concerning His promise, as some count slackness, but is longsuffering toward us, not willing that any should perish but that all should come to repentance."*
> 2 Peter 3:8-9

CHAPTER 4

THE CERTAINTY OF HIS RETURN

The Lord is coming at the appointed time. That is a definite and reliable fact. The question is — are we ready for His return?

While the "signs of the times" are evident for all to see, many will be surprised and shocked at the suddenness of it all.

> *"But the day of the Lord will come as a thief in the night,*
> *in which the heavens will pass away with a great noise,*
> *and the elements will melt with fervent heat;*
> *both the earth and the works that are in it*
> *will be burned up.*
> *Therefore, since all these things will be dissolved,*
> *what manner of persons ought you to be*
> *in holy conduct and godliness,*
> *looking for and hastening the coming of the day of God,*
> *because of which the heavens will be dissolved, being on fire,*
> *and the elements will melt with fervent heat?"*
> 2 Peter 3:10-12

Yes, the Promise of His Coming is sure and those who have an "understanding of the times" like the Sons of Issachar mentioned in 1 Chronicles 12:32, will find a conversation Jesus had with His disciples — recorded in Matthew chapter 24 — most enlightening.

During the course of that conversation, Jesus mentioned a number of signs that would precede His return.

Let's take a brief look at some of the Signs of the Times.

Chapter 5

Political Turmoil

*"And you will hear of wars and rumors of wars.
See that you are not troubled; for all these things must come to pass,
but the end is not yet.
For nation will rise against nation, and kingdom against kingdom."*
Matthew 24:6-7

War is nothing new to mankind. We have been involved in wars since the beginning of time and this is not something unique to our generation.

Jesus said it would be so... until the end times when war will escalate into a global battle involving all the nations and kingdoms of this world. We are watching it happen as our "Global Village" prepares itself for the greatest conflict this world has ever seen.

War is the hallmark of our generation. A study of wars since 500 B.C. shows a dramatic increase in recent years. The 20th Century SAW five major wars — World War I, World War II, the Korean War, Vietnam, and the Gulf War — with a death poll of 59,5 million according to the Academic American Encyclopaedia, Electron Version (Danbury, Conn Grolier, 1995). The 21st Century has fared no better.

Never has the world seen so much conflict on a global scale as it is experiencing at this present time. Nation is rising up against nation, and kingdom against kingdom and it is estimated that, of all the world conflicts since just 1990, all except three have been civil or ethnic.

Every day our news headlines tell us about trouble in Chechnya, Bosnia, Africa, and other parts of the world. Our hearts break as we watch little children, elderly people, and innocent citizens suffer dreadfully.

The Middle East is a powder keg just waiting to explode, as Iran and Iraq race to acquire more potent weapons and Israel struggles to keep her land. Everybody is involved as world rulers struggle to bring about some sort of fragile peace — and world citizens watch developments on their television screens.

The more men cry out for peace, the worse things seem to get. The words of Jesus are being literally fulfilled right before our eyes.

Chapter 6

The Explosion of Knowledge

About 2,500 years ago Daniel prophesied that the end times would see an unprecedented increase in travel and education.

> *"But you, Daniel, shut up the words, and seal the book*
> *until the time of the end;*
> *many shall run to and fro,*
> *and knowledge shall increase."*
> Daniel 12:4

It has been estimated that, if the whole of history could be condensed into just 24 hours, all the major discoveries would have happened in the last half-an-hour. That is awesome!

Men were riding horses at the beginning of this century — now they are planning excursions to outer space! The incredible developments in travel and education, with the advance of science and computers, are mind-boggling. Knowledge is increasing at such a pace that computers are out of date even before they leave the workshop!

Man is so clever he can make the deaf hear with the aid of science. The new "bionic ear" costs a small fortune, but it can reverse profound deafness. A South African family in Cape Town had one fitted in the ear of their little three-year-old. It cost around $800,000 ... and she hears perfectly. (South African Mercury. 3/10/1996).

The undeniable explosion of knowledge has certainly helped to escalate the war situation. The first World War, for example, introduced modern machine guns, tanks, heavy artillery and poison gas. World War Two produced mass destruction from the air and unleashed the awesome power of the atomic bomb, killing hundreds of thousands. The Cold War advanced missile technology and nuclear weapons capable of annihilating all human life on our planet and rocking the very earth on its axis.

An amazed world witnessed high-tech weapons reaching the limits of range, lethality and speed during the Gulf War. By the end of Desert Storm, according to the South African Mercury (8/10/1996) there were more than 3,000 computers in the Gulf, all linked to computers in the United States, 118,000 mobile satellite ground stations and 30,000 radio frequencies carrying 152 000 messages a day. Thirty million telephone calls were made to co-ordinate the air campaign alone. Control of information gave control of the battlefield demonstrating the unparalleled link between knowledge and power.

Hitler, Stalin, Mao Tse Tung, and scores of lesser dictators, have combined to make this period the bloodiest in human history.

There is more to come. The Lord said, when He looked at the Tower of Babel, that people, united in a common purpose, could achieve unbelievable things.

> *"And the Lord said, Indeed the people are one*
> *and they all have one language, and this is what they begin to do;*
> *now nothing that they propose to do will be withheld from them"*
> Genesis 11:6

Today we talk glibly about cloning animals and people, yet in spite of all our scientific advancement, mankind is sinking further and further into moral decline.

A believer was once asked why God (who claimed to be so powerful), did not stop all the wars and fighting. "Why should He," came the swift reply, "He didn't start them!"

War is here to stay. God has a very definite purpose in allowing men and nations to stubbornly fight it out. Not only is prophecy being fulfilled, but events are being set in motion that will culminate in the prophesied one-world system, dominated by a powerful world ruler.

Chapter 7

The Coming World Ruler

The world will find itself in such a mess eventually that they will cry out for "someone" to take control and bring peace.

Henri Spaak, early planner of the European Common Market and Secretary-General of NATO, is reported to have said: "We do not want another committee — we have too many already. What we want is a man of sufficient stature to hold the allegiance of all people, and to lift us out of the economic morass into which we are sinking. Send us such a man, and be he God or devil, we will receive him."

Such a man is waiting to be revealed. The Bible calls him the antichrist. He will be possessed by satan himself and is destined to rule the world for a period of seven years, called in scripture "The Great Tribulation."

Many Christians believe the Church will be removed from the earth at this time and believers will see the events leading up to his reign, but he will only be revealed once we are gone.

"For the mystery of lawlessness is already at work;
only He who now restrains will do so until He is taken out of the way.
And then the lawless one will be revealed,
whom the Lord will consume with the breath of His mouth

> *and destroy with the brightness of His coming."*
> 2 Thessalonians 2:7-8

This world ruler will bring a period of "pseudo peace" to the world at the beginning of his rule. Everyone will believe him to be the "Promised One" and will give him total allegiance.

Revelation 6:2 calls him the "conqueror on a white horse," counterfeiting the One described by John in Revelation 19:11-16.

> *"And I looked, and behold, a white horse.*
> *He who sat on it had a bow; and a crown was given to him,*
> *and he went out conquering and to conquer."*
> Revelation 6:2

Here is a description of the genuine Messiah, the Lord Jesus Christ.

> *"Now I saw heaven opened, and behold, a white horse.*
> *And He who sat on him was called Faithful and True,*
> *and in righteousness He judges and makes war.*
> *His eyes were like a flame of fire, and on His head were many crowns.*
> *He had a name written that no one knew except Himself.*
> *He was clothed with a robe dipped in blood,*
> *and His name is called The Word of God.*
> *And the armies in heaven, clothed in fine linen, white and clean,*
> *followed Him on white horses.*
> *Now out of His mouth goes a sharp sword,*
> *that with it He should strike the nations.*
> *And He Himself will rule them with a rod of iron.*
> *He Himself treads the winepress of the fierceness*
> *and wrath of Almighty God.*
> *And He has on His robe and on His thigh a name written:*

KING OF KINGS AND LORD OF LORDS."
Revelation 19:11-16

Scripture tells us that even the Jews will hail the antichrist as "Messiah"... until he reveals his true colours midway through his seven-year reign.

> *"He will oppose and will exalt himself over everything*
> *that is called God or is worshipped,*
> *so that he sets himself up in God's temple,*
> *proclaiming himself to be God."*
> 2 Thessalonians 2:4

The antichrist will allow the Nation of Israel to rebuild their Temple, but when it is complete he will enter it and declare himself to be God. Israel's eyes will be opened and that pseudo peace will be over as fresh efforts are made to exterminate and annihilate God's ancient people.

The Bible also tells us that we can expect three major things to happen in preparation for the reign of antichrist — the establishment of a one-world governmental system, a one-world religious system, and a one-world economic system.

CHAPTER 8

THE ONE-WORLD GOVERNMENT

Increased centralization of world financial and political power is a prelude to the soon-coming world political system seen by John the Apostle in his vision around 80 A.D. and recorded by him in the book of Revelation.

> *"Then I stood on the sand of the sea.*
> *And I saw a beast rising up out of the sea,*
> *having seven heads and ten horns,*
> *and on his horns ten crowns,*
> *and on his heads a blasphemous name"*
> Revelation 13:1

We notice two things in particular, about this "beast – it has ten horns and seven heads. Each horn has a crown, symbolizing ten kingdoms or nations in an end-time coalition. Seven heads are closely connected. Could they be the "brains" directing the nations?

We are watching a coalition of nations form in our generation that should make every thinking person sit up and take notice. Called the European Union or Common Market, it is currently made up of a number of nations, including Austria, Finland, France, Germany, Greece, Ireland, Italy, Netherlands, Portugal, Spain, Sweden, the United Kingdom, and Benelux (comprising Belgium, Denmark and Luxembourg).

And right behind the scenes, the extremely powerful and influential "Group of Seven" directs the finances of the world. These are the leaders of the seven biggest industrial democracies of the world and they have a finger in every pie.

The book of Daniel gives us some more information concerning this end-time coalition.

Caniel chapter two tells us about a dream King Nebuchadnezzar of Babylon had concerning a very large statue. Daniel was called upon to interpret the dream and the Lord told him what it was all about.

The dream referred to four kingdoms, he informed Nebuchadnezzar — his own Babylonian kingdom (head of gold), followed by three more world empires. History tells us who they are — the Persian/Median (chest and arms of silver), the Greek (bronze belly and thigh), and the Roman (iron legs).

A fifth kingdom, closely aligned to the fourth — a revived Roman Empire in the last days — would be made up of ten kingdoms ... some weak and some very strong (ten toes of iron and baked clay).

In confirmation of this, God gave Daniel two personal visions and explained their contents.

The first is recorded in Daniel chapter seven. He saw four great beasts, again representing four world empires. He was particularly fascinated by the fourth because it had ten horns.

While he was thinking about these horns, he noticed "another horn, a little one" with "eyes like the eyes of a man and a mouth that spoke boastfully" (7:8). This horn destroyed three of the original ten horns and dominated the others.

Daniel recorded the explanation the Lord gave him in 7:23-27:

> *"Thus he said: 'The fourth beast shall be a fourth kingdom on earth, which shall be different from all other kingdoms and shall devour the whole earth, trample it and break it in pieces.*
> *The ten horns are ten kings who shall arise from this kingdom.*
> *And another shall rise after them;*
> *He shall be different from the first ones, and shall subdue three kings.*
> *He shall speak pompous words against the Most High,*
> *Shall persecute the saints of the Most High,*
> *and shall intend to change times and law.*
> *Then the saints shall be given into his hand for*
> *a time and times and half a time. '*
> *But the court shall be seated, and they shall take away his dominion, to consume and destroy it forever.*
> *Then the kingdom and dominion,*
> *And the greatness of the kingdoms under the whole heaven, shall be given to the people, the saints of the Most High. His kingdom is an everlasting kingdom,*
> *and all dominions shall serve and obey Him.'"*
> Daniel 7:23-27

This end-time coalition of nations will, we are told, persecute God's people (the Jewish nation) for three-and-a-half years. We have already taken note that midway through the seven-year period, known as the Great Tribulation, the antichrist will reveal his true colours and all hell will be let loose against Israel.

Daniel's second vision is recorded in chapter eight of his book. It has the same basic elements, but this time he is given the names of the future empires and he writes them down hundreds of years before they came into existence! Daniel actually mentions the names of Persia and Greece. At that time Greece was not a world empire and it was only when Alexander the Great took control, that this specific prophecy was fulfilled.

> *"Now, as he was speaking with me, I was in a deep sleep*
> *with my face to the ground; but he touched me, and stood me upright.*
> *And he said, "Look, I am making known to you*
> *what shall happen in the latter time of the indignation;*
> *for at the appointed time the end shall be.*
> *The ram which you saw, having the two horns—they are*
> *the kings of Media and Persia.*
> *And the male goat is the kingdom of Greece.*
> *The large horn that is between its eyes is the first king.*
> *As for the broken horn and the four that stood up in its place,*
> *four kingdoms shall arise out of that nation, but not with its power.*
> *And in the latter time of their kingdom,*
> *When the transgressors have reached their fullness,*
> *A king shall arise, Having fierce features,*
> *Who understands sinister schemes.*
> *His power shall be mighty, but not by his own power;*
> *He shall destroy fearfully, And shall prosper and thrive;*
> *He shall destroy the mighty, and also the holy people.*
> *Through his cunning He shall cause deceit to prosper under his rule;*
> *And he shall exalt himself in his heart.*
> *He shall destroy many in their prosperity.*
> *He shall even rise against the Prince of princes;*
> *But he shall be broken without human means.*
> *And the vision of the evenings and mornings which was told is true;*
> *Therefore seal up the vision, or it refers to many days in the future."*
> *Daniel 8:18-26*

The angel who shared this vision with Daniel emphasized that these are end-time events.

> *"So he came near where I stood, and when he came I was afraid*
> *and fell on my face; but he said to me,*

"Understand, son of man, that the vision refers to the time of the end."
Daniel 8:17

Are we watching the revived Roman Empire beginning to take shape in preparation for the final world government? Keep in mind that antichrist's government will consist of ten nations or groups of nations.

Does it surprise you to know that the world has already been organized into ten regions for trade purposes?

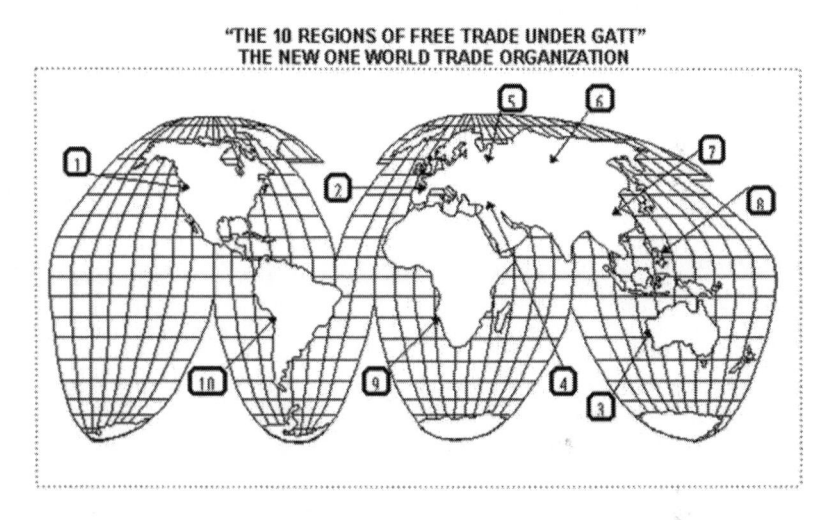

"THE 10 REGIONS OF FREE TRADE UNDER GATT"
THE NEW ONE WORLD TRADE ORGANIZATION

That the European Union has roots in Rome is a fact of history. Jean Monnet founded the European Economic Community (EEC), with its headquarters in Brussels, Belgium on March 25, 1957, with the signing of the Treaty of Rome. Its successor — the European Union — was subsequently brought into being in November 1993, with the ratification of the Maastricht Treaty.

The Second Treaty of Rome signed on October 29, 2004. This was followed by the Treaty of Lisbon on December 13, 2007 and was finally ratified and signed into law on December 1, 2009

This political union will effectively become a United States of Europe, with its own currency and government as it evolves into an undisputed world power.

Forbes magazine (April 1988) said: "By the year 2010, the entity that is Europe will be number one in the world economy. The U.S. will be second, China third, and Japan fourth."

It is not surprising, therefore, that we read headlines like "New EC currency unit poses challenge to mighty US dollar" (South African Mercury dated 6/12/1991) or "Europe poised to take economic control of the world."

"Future historians," says George Gordon of the London Daily Mail, "will record that the 21st century belonged to Europe."

Leon Trotsky, the Russian Communist leader, wrote something very interesting comment in 1918. He said: "The task of the proletariat is to create a United States of Europe, as a foundation for the United States of the World." (Bolshevism and World Peace)

Mikhail Gorbachev foretold a global government in 1992. He told an outdoor crowd of thousands in America that an awareness of the need for some kind of global government is gaining ground "one in which all members of the world community would take part."

World government thinking is not foreign to us and we are familiar with the term "New World Order". In May 1992, one South African newspaper carried an article entitled "Africa lags behind new world order."

The President at that time, F.W. de Klerk, was quoted as saying that Africa was lagging behind the current global economic realignment and still largely lacked a sense of common destiny.

South African President Nelson Mandela told a joint sitting of the United States Congress on October 6, 1994, that: "It is our deeply held belief that the *New World Order* that is in the making must focus on the creation of a world of democracy, peace and prosperity for all humanity".

Former American President George Bush, speaking of the Persian Gulf crisis, said on September 11, 1990: "Out of these troubled times, a New World Order can emerge, under a United Nations that performs as envisioned by its founders."

Two weeks later Soviet Foreign Minister, Eduard Shevardnadze, speaking at the United Nations, said: "Iraq has committed an unprovoked act of aggression... an act of terrorism which has been perpetrated against the emerging New World Order."

The New World Order is an attempt to create a world government, which unites capitalists and communists, and has the ability to over-rule the decisions of duly elected governments.

It is actively promoted by a loose network of organisations motivated by a similar system of beliefs, known as the New Age Movement. Their Fourth Provisional World Parliament met in Innsbruck, Austria, from June 26 to July 6, 1996, and claims to represent nearly 600 organisations from 95 countries, comprising approximately 20 million individuals. Planning for a world government is well under way.

The South African Mercury (February 20, 1992) posed the question: "Sounds neat and tidy, but who's in charge?"

Bible lovers can tell them who is going to *take* charge!

The revived Roman Empire is already here. How long before the World Government takes control? We are watching it happen in our generation!

CHAPTER 9

THE ONE-WORLD RELIGION

Global war resulting in a Global government will also see another development — a religious system that will support the one-world government and the antichrist with fanatical fervour.

In his vision, recorded in Revelation chapter 13, John describes what he saw.

> *'Then I saw another beast coming up out of the earth, and he had two horns like a lamb and spoke like a dragon. And he exercises all the authority of the first beast in his presence, and causes the earth and those who dwell in it to worship the first beast, whose deadly wound was healed. He performs great signs, so that he even makes fire come down from heaven on the earth in the sight of men. And he deceives those who dwell on the earth by those signs which he was granted to do in the sight of the beast, telling those who dwell on the earth to make an image to the beast who was wounded by the sword and lived. He was granted power to give breath to the image of the beast, that the image of the beast should both speak and cause as many as would not worship the image of the beast to be killed."*
> Revelation 13:11-15

Here we are told that another governmental system would take its place in the last days. This time it is a religious system with "horns like a lamb," but speaking with the authority of the dragon himself... identified clearly as satan by the Bible (Revelation chapter 12 and other scriptures).

Notice that this dragon has two horns, speaking of two major religious systems that will unite in these days.

The object of their worship will be the World Ruler, a man totally possessed by satan.

> *"The coming of the lawless one is according to the working of Satan,*
> *with all power, signs, and lying wonders,*
> *and with all unrighteous deception among those who perish,*
> *because they did not receive the love of the truth,*
> *that they might be saved."*
> 2 Thessalonians 2:9-10

The culmination of their worship will be satan himself.

> *"So they worshiped the dragon who gave authority to the beast;*
> *and they worshiped the beast, saying, "Who is like the beast?*
> *Who is able to make war with him?"*
> Revelation 13:4

John alludes to an incident in the life of the World Ruler that is most interesting. He says that one of the heads of the beast seemed to have had a fatal wound, but the fatal wound appears to have been miraculously healed.

> *"And I saw one of his heads as if it had been mortally wounded,*
> *and his deadly wound was healed.*
> *And all the world marveled and followed the beast."*
> Revelation 13:3

This counterfeit resurrection of the beast *"who was wounded by the sword and lived"* (Revelation 13:14) will convince the nations that he is indeed the "Risen Lord."

Those who use miracles as a yardstick for judgment would do well to take note.

The religious system will embrace the whole world.

> *"All who dwell on the earth will worship him,*
> *whose names have not been written in the Book of Life of the Lamb*
> *slain from the foundation of the world.*
> *If anyone has an ear, let him hear,"*
> Revelation 13:8-9

Those who commit themselves to the Lord Jesus Christ during this time will pay the ultimate price. John talks about them in Revelation 9

> *"When He opened the fifth seal, I saw under the altar*
> *the souls of those who had been slain for the word of God*
> *and for the testimony which they held.*
> *And they cried with a loud voice, saying,*
> *"How long, O Lord, holy and true, until You judge*
> *and avenge our blood on those who dwell on the earth?"*
> *Then a white robe was given to each of them;*
> *and it was said to them that they should rest a little while longer,*
> *until both the number of their fellow servants and their brethren,*
> *who would be killed as they were, was completed."*
> Revelation 6:9-11

The question we must ask ourselves now is whether a religious coalition is taking place in our generation, embracing all "faiths" and moving towards a common destiny. Are there any two particular groups that stand out above the others in this quest for unity?

Without doubt, the answer is YES to both these questions.

The New Age Movement is very busy indeed promoting the "Interfaith" concept and New Age philosophy and theology are infiltrating all religious groups, especially a backslidden "church."

By means of New Age ecumenical peace prayer services, people are taught to believe that through prayer we can all be one — irrespective of truth and falsehood, good and evil — Christians, Muslims, Hindus, Buddhists, occultists, animists, satanists, whatever. The Age of Aquarius has arrived and all division must be done away with. God and man, saint and sinner, Christian and heathen... all must become one harmonious whole, living in peace.

The New Age movement is also behind the "Peace Poles," tall obelisks with lettering in Perspex, which reads: "May peace prevail on earth." Over 60,000 of them have reportedly been planted all over the world.

South Africa has one on Table Mountain and another in Bloemfontein. All religions are invited to share in the "peace prayers" offered during the planting ceremonies.

One can't help wondering what Elijah would have had to say to our generation! He refused to pray with the prophets of Baal in his day.

> *"Elijah came to all the people, and said,*
> *"How long will you falter between two opinions?*
> *If the Lord is God, follow Him; but if Baal, follow him."*
> *But the people answered him not a word.*
> *Then Elijah said to the people,*
> *"I alone am left a prophet of the Lord;*
> *but Baal's prophets are four hundred and fifty men.*
> *Therefore let them give us two bulls;*
> *and let them choose one bull for themselves,*
> *cut it in pieces, and lay it on the wood, but put no fire under it;*

> *and I will prepare the other bull, and lay it on the wood,*
> *but put no fire under it.*
> *Then you call on the name of your gods,*
> *and I will call on the name of the Lord;*
> *and the God who answers by fire, He is God."*
> 1 Kings 18:21-24

God demonstrated that day that He is the unrivalled God of the Universe.

> *"I am the Lord, and there is no other;*
> *There is no God besides Me."*
> Isaiah 45:5a

The quest for unity is on at any price. Leaders of the New Age movement, frustrated at the increasing resistance from "born-again" Christians, are reported to have declared in their 13-point Plan for World Peace that Christians who resist the plan will be dealt with. If necessary, they are to be "exterminated" and the world "purified" (Principle 13 of the Plan).

The Lord Jesus Christ's claim to be the ONLY WAY to God infuriates New Age proponents.

> *"Jesus said to him, "I am the way, the truth, and the life.*
> *No one comes to the Father except through Me."*
> John 14:6

The Early Church believed Him and Peter, filled with the Holy Spirit, declared emphatically:

> *"Nor is there salvation in any other, for there is no other Name*
> *under heaven given among men by which we must be saved."*
> Acts 4:12

One of the two major religious groups involved in the "interfaith" concept is today's modernistic, humanistic, apology for the Church of Jesus Christ, very graphically described in Revelation 3:14-22. It is the Laodicean Church symbolizing elements of the last Church age.

> *"And to the angel of the church of the Laodiceans write, "These things says the Amen, the Faithful and True Witness, the Beginning of the creation of God:*
> *"I know your works, that you are neither cold nor hot. I could wish you were cold or hot. So then, because you are lukewarm, and neither cold nor hot, I will vomit you out of My mouth. Because you say, "I am rich, have become wealthy, and have need of nothing'—and do not know that you are wretched, miserable, poor, blind, and naked—*
> *I counsel you to buy from Me gold refined in the fire, that you may be rich and white garments, that you may be clothed, that the shame of your nakedness may not be revealed; and anoint your eyes with eye salve, that you may see. As many as I love, I rebuke and chasten. Therefore be zealous and repent. Behold, I stand at the door and knock. If anyone hears My voice and opens the door, I will come in to him and dine with him, and he with Me. To him who overcomes I will grant to sit with Me on My throne, as I also overcame and sat down with My Father on His throne. He who has an ear, let him hear what the Spirit says to the churches."*
> Revelation 3:14-22

That is the Lord's opinion of those who name His Name, but refuse to acknowledge Him as Sovereign Lord.

What a joy to know that there will always be the true Church of Jesus Christ, kept by the Power of God and standing firm in His Name. Found in every denomination and walk of life, these are the people who love the Lord and serve Him with all their heart and mind and soul and strength.

The Lord has a special word of encouragement for them:

> *"I know your works. See, I have set before you an open door,*
> *and no one can shut it; for you have a little strength,*
> *have kept My word, and have not denied My name.*
> *Indeed I will make those of the synagogue of Satan,*
> *who say they are Jews and are not, but lie—*
> *indeed I will make them come and worship before your feet,*
> *and to know that I have loved you. 1*
> *Because you have kept My command to persevere,*
> *I also will keep you from the hour of trial which shall come*
> *upon the whole world, to test those who dwell on the earth.*
> *Behold, I am coming quickly! Hold fast what you have,*
> *that no one may take your crown"*
> Revelation 3:8-11

But it's the end-time apostate "church" that interests us at this point. About to enter into an adulterous and idolatrous union with those who absolutely refuse to acknowledge Jesus Christ as LORD OF LORDS AND KING OF KINGS, the powerful (so-called) Christian church is in big trouble as it stands on the threshold of losing its identity as "Christian," a title given to early believers in Antioch during the first Century A.D.

> *"And when he had found him, he brought him to Antioch. So it was that for*
> *a whole year they assembled with the church*
> *and taught a great many people.*
> *And the disciples were first called Christians in Antioch."*
> Acts 11:26

The challenge of Christ is as relevant for our generation as it has ever been.

> *"Therefore whoever confesses Me before men,*
> *him I will also confess before My Father who is in heaven.*
> *But whoever denies Me before men,*
> *him I will also deny before My Father who is in heaven."*
> *Matthew 10:32-33*

Sadly, its leaders deny that the Bible is the Word of God, declaring it should be rewritten so that God will not be seen as only the property of certain religions. The deity of Christ, His virgin birth ("pictorial theology"), His death, resurrection, ascension and return are rejected outright. The Biblical description of Heaven and Hell are described as "crude medieval images" that don't belong to modern times.

You can believe anything you like... so long as you don't believe in the "Living Word" — the Lord Jesus Christ — and the "Written Word" — the Bible!

The other group that is very involved in the interfaith movement is Islam. The South African Daily News (24/9/1992), reported that the Islamic Relief Agency (ISRA) were behind the interfaith peace march in Durban on September 25 and that they had issued an invitation to the general public to join their march.

Islam is becoming increasingly militant and powerful in our generation.

The victory of the Taliban fighters in Afghanistan is a case in point. The public hanging of Afghanistan's last communist president, Najibullah, and the restrictions on women and girls caused a great deal of anxiety in the country. Girls were no longer allowed to attend school and some social programmes had to be suspended because female aid workers were forced to stay at home. Soldiers guarded the mosques during prayers .to ensure the people pray five times a day as decreed by the Taliban regime... or face punishment. (South African Mercury 8/10/1996).

Taliban proclamations identified Mullah Omar as Amir ul-Monineen, an Arabic term meaning "prince of the believers." This title goes back more than 1000 years to disciples of Mohammed and its use, implying that he envisaged himself as a leader for Muslims beyond Afghanistan. It shocked Muslims all over the world.

The Christian Church, claiming its roots in Abraham, via Isaac — the promised son that produced the Messianic Line — is being forced to acknowledge the descendants of Abraham via Ishmael.

"Isaac" and "Ishmael" must make peace in the last days if they are to share in the antichrist's short reign of pseudo peace. What else can they do but unite?

It's happening already! A special Eid message from Cardinal Francis Arinze, president of the Secretariat of the Holy See for relations with believers of others religions, was relayed to Durban's Muslim community in South Africa by the Roman Catholic Archbishop of Durban.

It read in part: "During the month of Ramadan, you have shown, by prayer and fasting, your faith in God and your submission to His holy will. This faith in the One God, Living and True, a faith which is the heritage of all spiritual children of Abraham, the father of believers, UNITES US as brothers and sisters in God and encourages us to work together for solidarity, justice and peace among all people."

Our generation is observing this unholy marriage, without realizing its implications.

CHAPTER 10

THE ONE WORLD ECONOMY

If there is anything that should convince the most sceptical among us that we are living in the last of the "last days," it is the prophecies concerning the world economy. Nobody can miss what is happening. When it comes to money, we are all involved.

John prophesied that the world government will use the world religious system to indoctrinate the inhabitants of the earth and persuade them to participate in the global economy.

> *"He [The False Prophet] causes all, both small and great, rich and poor, free and slave, to receive a mark on their right hand or on their foreheads, and that no one may buy or sell except one who has the mark or the name of the beast, or the number of his name. Here is wisdom. Let him who has understanding calculate the number of the beast, for it is the number of a man: His number is 666."*
> Revelation 13:16-18

This prophecy has had Christians guessing for centuries. It is only in the computer age — our generation again! — that we are beginning to make sense of it.

When the huge E.C. computer (nicknamed "the beast" by the media) was inaugurated, one of the leaders, Dr. Eldeman, suggested that by using a three six digital units, the entire world could be assigned a working credit card number.

The first six numbers of our I.D. would incorporate our birth date (South African's already have some experience of this... and we are not alone).

The second series of six numbers denote our location. In 1977 photographs taken from satellites, and subsequently updated, were used to divide the entire world and major cities into a complete mesh block system. These figures will specify the precise street where we live, it would appear.

The third series of six numbers links all the vital information together in a unique I.D. number.

This is not fiction — it is actually happening and the success of the "cashless society" hinges on it.

Cash is going out of fashion (Daily News, Friday, 26/7/1996) and soon there will be no need to have money. The "electronic purse" — a "smart card" revolution — is set to sweep South Africa according to the Sunday Times, Business Times, March 38, 1993. It is already being used in many parts of the world.

The smart card is like a plastic credit card, less than one millimetre thick. It has a microcomputer chip embedded in it with as much computing power as the personal computers of the early 1980's. It will be able to carry information, secure identity details, and be used for all financial transactions.

Because smart cards will replace cash, legislation may be required shortly to force financial institutions to accommodate smart-card readers in all ATMs (automated teller networks) in a hurry, according to press reports.

Physical money is almost history! Which is why banks are charging ridiculous prices for financial transactions involving cash money and advertising great savings for those who make use of the electronic facilities.

"The end of money is nigh"..."Safer, cashless shopping is here with smart card"... "Cyber shopping takes off"... "Smart Card paves way to cashless society"... "Cards that put paid to coins and vandals" — these are just a few headlines picked at random from various newspapers.

"Cybercash" has already become a reality on the Internet. All you have to do is visit the CyberCash Web site and download an empty electronic wallet onto your computer hard drive. The software programme acts like an ATM, making it possible to transfer money from your banking account into your electronic wallet... and you're ready to go shopping! The company's CyberCoin system will allow online "micro transactions" as small as an American quarter.

Impossible to implement among the uneducated and illiterate masses? Antichrist will find a way, says John... small and great, rich and poor, free and slave... everybody will have to co-operate or face the consequences. It's that simple.

> *"He causes all, both small and great, rich and poor, free and slave, to receive a mark on their right hand or on their foreheads, and that no one may buy or sell except one who has the mark or the name of the beast, or the number of his name."*
> Revelation 13:16-17

The smart card is just the beginning. John tells us in Revelation 13:16 that every individual will eventually have a microchip in their body – on their right hand or on their forehead".

This idea is not new to us either. Our generation already puts these in domestic animals, fish, race-horses and motor-cars. The "Identipet," an implantable microchip, is available at your local vet. The SPCA, vets and police have scanners, which enable them to identify your animal immediately.

A secular computer magazine carried an article as early as May, 1992, posing the question: Why carry cards when an implant will do the trick?

The technology is here already. The "identification transponder" is smaller than a grain of rice and implanting it just beneath the skin of the right hand or forehead is now a practical reality. How close are we to the rule of antichrist?

The U.S.A. "Womb to Tomb" health care programme has bills before Congress at the present time that will allow them to inject a microchip into children at the time of birth for identification purposes.

The President of the United States, under the "Emigration of Control Act of 1986" Section 100, already has the authority to deem whatever type of identification is necessary... whether it be an invisible tattoo or electronic media under the skin.

The Washington Times ran an article entitled "High-tech national tattoo" on October 11, 1993, describing an identification system made by the Hughes Aircraft Company that you couldn't lose — the syringe implantable transponder.

It is said to be an "ingenious, safe, inexpensive, foolproof and permanent method of identification using radio waves."

The Hughes Missiles Systems Company already uses microchips to track aircraft and vehicles. But can people be tracked?

The new low-orbiting satellites, such as the 66 satellites that Motorola putt up in conjunction with the Russians, can track certain microchips. It was used to track military personnel in the Iraq war and it is envisaged that this chip will eventually be used for life-long identification of human beings.

The one-world government... the one-world religious system... the one-word economy... everything is ready! It will just take the revelation of the antichrist to put it all in motion.

Current events in the financial world are causing great concern as one Nation after another faces bankrupcy.

How close are we to the last phase of world history? And how much closer are we to the Rapture?

The generation that sees all these signs being fulfilled, said Jesus in that incredible conversation on the Mount of Olives, will also see His Return.

Chapter 11

The Call To Be Ready

*"Therefore you also be ready,
for the Son of Man is coming at an hour you do not expect."
Matthew 24:44*

It is vital to be ready for the Coming of the Lord. In that instant, when the people of God are caught up to meet Him in the clouds, there will be no opportunity to get right with Him. Those who are left behind will have to face the reign of antichrist and the terrible trauma the world will find itself in, culminating in the Battle of Armageddon and the Visible Return of Christ with all His saints.

That will be a day of pure terror for the UNBELIEVER.

*"And the kings of the earth, the great men, the rich men, the commanders,
the mighty men, every slave and every free man,
hid themselves in the caves and in the rocks of the mountains,
and said to the mountains and rocks,
Fall on us and hide us from the face of Him who sits on the throne
and from the wrath of the Lamb!
For the great day of His wrath has come, and who is able to stand?"
Revelation 6:15-17*

It is not too late now. The Lord still stands at the door of every heart and knocks.

> *"Behold, I stand at the door and knock.*
> *If anyone hears My voice and opens the door,*
> *I will come in to him and dine with him, and he with Me"*
> . Revelation 3:20

Receive the Lord as your Saviour right this moment! There is a special prayer you can pray following this chapter. Turn there now. Do not delay.

For the "RELIGIOUS PERSON," this is the time to examine the reality of your faith. Religion is not enough — CHRIST ALONE is THE WAY to Heaven.

> *"Examine yourselves as to whether you are in the faith.*
> *Test yourselves. Do you not know yourselves,*
> *that Jesus Christ is in you? —unless indeed you are* disqualified."
> 2 Corinthians 13:5

Ask yourself whether the LIFE OF GOD is coursing through your being. God has no "still-born babies" — who show no sign of spiritual life, no hunger for His Word, no growth in grace and the knowledge of Jesus Christ, no beautiful aroma of Christ in their lives. Neither does He have any "grandchildren" — those who "piggyback" on the experience of others.

Only those who are truly the sons and daughters of the Lord are part of His true Church.

> *"But as many as received Him, to them He gave the right to become children of God, to those who believe in His name:who were born, not of blood, nor of the will of the flesh, nor of the will of man, but of God."*
> John 1:12-13

Often we talk about the building as the Church. The truth is that the Church only worships in the building!

For the CARELESS UNPREPARED BELIEVER, it will be a day of great loss as the "fire test" is put to our lives.

> *"For no other foundation can anyone lay than that which is laid, which is Jesus Christ. Now if anyone builds on this foundation with gold, silver, precious stones, wood, hay, straw, each one's work will become clear; for the Day will declare it, because it will be revealed by fire; and the fire will test each one's work, of what sort it is. If anyone's work which he has built on it endures, he will receive a reward. If anyone's work is burned, he will suffer loss; but he himself will be saved, yet so as through fire."*
> 1 Corinthians 3:11-15

Now is the time to take stock and to prepare your heart for His Return.

> *"Therefore, since all these things will be dissolved, what manner of persons ought you to be in holy conduct and godliness, looking for and hastening the coming of the day of God, because of which the heavens will be dissolved, being on fire, and the elements will melt with fervent heat?"*
> 2 Peter 3:11-12

Jesus concluded His conversation with a number of illustrative parable, among them the story of the ten virgins. Half were "religious" and missed the coming of the Bridegroom. "I tell you the truth, I DON'T KNOW YOU", He said, when they pleaded for Him to open the door (Matthew 25:12).

Half were ready and waiting, expectant and pure... and when the cry rang out at midnight: "Here's the Bridegroom! Come out to meet Him!" — their hearts were prepared.

For EXPECTANT BELIEVERS with their eyes on the clouds... it is a day of glory!

> *"Beloved, now we are children of God; and it has not yet been revealed what we shall be, but we know that when He is revealed, we shall be like Him, for we shall see Him as He is. And everyone who has this hope in Him purifies himself, just as He is pure."*
> 1 John 3:2-3

What a day that will be! The fulfilment of our deepest longing... the culmination of our greatest hopes... the completion of our highest joy.

Many years ago a Man of God preached the Word on a beach in Durban. He stood there in his purple ministerial vest and his face shone as he looked up at the sky. "Every morning", he said, "the first thing I do when I wake up is go to the window, draw the curtains and look up at the clouds. Every day I ask myself: Could today be the day Jesus comes? I try to live every minute of my day with that thought in mind."

That made an impression on my young life that has lasted through the years. I can't keep my eyes off the clouds either!

> *" He who testifies to these things says, "Surely I am coming quickly." Amen. Even so, come, Lord Jesus!"*
> Revelation 22:20

A Special Prayer For Those Who Need Christ

Heavenly Father,

Right now, I come in the Name of the Lord Jesus Christ and acknowledge before You that I am a sinner — — hopelessly lost and powerless to save myself.

I recognise that Jesus Christ paid the supreme price for my sin and I am grateful.

Today, Lord, I ask You to come into my life and cleanse me thoroughly from sin,

Wash me with Your Precious Blood that I might be whiter than snow.

Forgive my sin and cause me to be re-born into Your Eternal Family.

I thank You for hearing me today and answering my prayer as I respond to Your Voice and open the door of my heart to You.

Please create in me a strong desire for Your Word and a passionate longing for Your Return.

In Jesus' Name.

Amen.

If you have prayed this prayer today and meant it with all your heart, please email me at the address below and share your testimony. I would love to hear from you.

About The Author

Val Waldeck, a well-known South African author, international Bible teacher and conference speaker, has written a number of books and writes regular columns in JOY, a major South African National Christian magazine. She was awarded the prestigious South African Writer's Circle "Writer of the Year" award in 2001 and 2002.

Val has been in fulltime Christian ministry since December 1973. She graduated from the Bible Institute of South Africa in 1972 and holds a Diploma in Theology with the University of London and a Doctorate in Theology with Teamwork International.

Contact Val:

Val Waldeck
Email: val@valwaldeck.com
www.valwaldeck.com – Reaching Our Generation One Book at a Time

DISCLAIMER

This publication is designed to provide condensed information. It is not intended to reprint all the information that is otherwise available, but instead to complement, amplify and supplement other texts. You are urged to read all the available material, learn as much as possible and tailor the information to your individual needs.

Every effort has been made to make this publication as complete and as accurate as possible. However, there may be mistakes, both typographical and in content. Therefore, this text should be used only as a general guide and not as the ultimate source of information.

The purpose of this publication is to educate. The author shall have neither liability nor responsibility to any person or entity with respect to any loss or damage caused, or alleged to have been caused, directly or indirectly, by the information contained in this publication.

More Books by Val

Visit www.valwaldeck.com for details of all Val's books

Printed in Great Britain
by Amazon